PRAISE FOR
REVVED!

"*REVVED!* is the perfect interconnected follow-up to *FISH!* The three levels of caring are beautifully embedded in a compelling story—which shows how through the power of choice we can master our own emotions and actions—all of which reinforces the saying, 'I don't care how much you know until I know how much you care.'"

—STEPHEN R. COVEY, author,
The 7 Habits of Highly Effective People and
The 8th Habit: From Effectiveness to Greatness

"*REVVED!* by Harry Paul and Ross Reck, presents an exciting new approach to energizing and motivating people to bring out the best in themselves and others. Read it, enjoy, and apply!"

—KEN BLANCHARD, coauthor,
The One Minute Manager and *The Secret*

"Look out! This is no ordinary book you hold in your hands. *REVVED!* is a tool for extraordinary performance in work and in life. It is a catalyst to turn on your innovative mind and tone up your creative mindset. It won't take much time to read, but its impact will last for all time."

—NIDO R. QUBEIN, President,
High Point University and
Chairman, Great Harvest Bread Company

"This is a super book—a must read! Learn how to recapture your caring, compassionate 'hugging' self and share the story of *REVVED!* with your associates and family."

—JACK MITCHELL, CEO,
Mitchells/Richards/Marshs and author of the
best-selling book *Hug Your Customers*

"What you give is what you get. Give others something great and then enjoy the benefits of greatness all around you! This book will show you how!"

—TOM MORRIS, author,
If Harry Potter Ran General Electric

"*REVVED!* is a very inspirational and quick read—easy to remember and follow. It's a book I will pick up and read again and again whenever I feel the energy level in my work unit starting to slip, because I know it works!"

— JODY ROBERTSON, Vice President, Wells Fargo Bank

"I took delight in reading *REVVED!* It's a really fun read that explicitly mirrors what I live and breathe each day. Truly caring about people is what drives their performance to the next level. *REVVED!* works for me, and it will work for you!"

—MARY BETH GALEY, Director,
Customer Care, Honeywell

"In my travels with *FISH!*, I have heard many sad stories about coworkers who seem to be dedicated to their own dissatisfaction; to their detriment and to the detriment of the firm. Thanks to Harry Paul and Ross Reck, who have brilliantly captured the antecedent conditions leading to a crusty worker, I now have something positive to suggest. That suggestion is *REVVED!*"

—STEPHEN C. LUNDIN, coauthor,
Top Performer and the *FISH!* series of books

"It really is a simple recipe for success. *REVVED!* makes you look in the mirror and see all of the missed opportunities to *Blow them away. REVVED!* is a must read for the first-time manager AND the experienced manager. Harry Paul and Ross Reck have created a three-step process that will stand the test of time. *REVVED!* will definitely be added to our management curriculum. I don't think I will ever get tired of hearing, 'Is there anything else I can do for you?'"

—PETER MARCHESINI, Vice President,
Training and Development, Ventiv Health

"*REVVED!* is a practical reflection of the key elements needed to motivate people to achieve their moments of magnificence. A pick-it-up-again-and-again book with practical examples that reminds us of the power of motivated people."

—GARRY RIDGE, President and CEO,
WD-40 Company

REVVED!

AN **INCREDIBLE** WAY TO REV UP
YOUR WORKPLACE AND **ACHIEVE**
AMAZING RESULTS

Harry Paul & Ross Reck, Ph.D.

McGRAW-HILL

New York Chicago San Francisco Lisbon London Madrid Mexico City
Milan New Delhi San Juan Seoul Singapore Sydney Toronto

The McGraw·Hill Companies

McGraw-Hill books are available at special quantity discounts to use as premiums and sales promotions, or for use in corporate training programs. For more information, please write to the Director of Special Sales, Professional Publishing, McGraw-Hill, Two Penn Plaza, New York, NY 10121-2298. Or contact your local bookstore.

Revved! is in no way authorized, endorsed by, or affiliated with ChartHouse International Learning Corporation, the creator of the Fish! Products.

Poem on p.12 is from Og Mandino, *Greatest Salesman in the World,* Hollywood, Fla.: Frederick Fell Publishers, 1968, p. 79.

 This book is printed on recycled, acid-free paper containing a minimum of 50% recycled de-inked fiber.

PREFACE

During the past 20-plus years, the two of us have delivered more than 1,000 lectures to corporations, small businesses, government agencies, nonprofit institutions, social organizations, service clubs, and universities in the United States, Canada, Europe, Asia, South America, and Mexico.

As we recently reflected on these experiences, one of the things that struck us was the amount of confusion that surrounds the act of caring about others. While most people quickly admit that caring about others is a good thing to do, they fail to appreciate two very important aspects of caring: how huge the return is that comes back to you from caring and how quickly your personal and professional lives can change for the better once you start.

Revved! introduces three easy steps that will show you how to maximize the return that comes back to you from caring. *Winning Them Over* shows you how to get others excited about going the extra mile for you, *Blowing Them Away* shows you how to take that excitement to the next level, and *Keeping Them Revved!* shows you how to sustain that high level of excitement indefinitely. As you put these three steps into practice, your success at work will immediately begin to skyrocket and your personal life will thrive as never before.

Harry Paul
Ross Reck

8-21-06

ACKNOWLEDGMENTS

There are many people involved in getting a book ready for publication, and we feel that there are several that we must single out:

Julia Woods, President, Professional Division, McGraw-Hill Ryerson, who inspired this book with a suggestion during a seminar.

Reverend Lana Neighbors, Hospice Chaplain, whose sermon freed up the mental energy necessary to write this book.

Marcia Reck, Ross's wife, for her willingness to proofread on demand throughout the duration of this project.

Mary Paul, Harry's wife, for her feedback and steadfast support for this project and encouraging him to take the *FISH!* project on when he was wavering.

Cheryl Hornyan, our friend, who provided proofreading assistance during the early phases of this project.

Tom Spain, for his editorial help during the early stages of the manuscript.

Margret McBride, our great agent, and her fantastic staff: Donna DeGutis, Faye Atchison, and Anne Bomke.

The extraordinary team at McGraw-Hill, especially Mary Glenn, Jeffrey Krames, and Ruth Mannino for their help in shaping this book and Philip Ruppel for his publishing vision. Also, a special thanks to the *Revved!* marketing and sales group.

ONE!

TUESDAY MORNING, the Chicago suburbs: Katie Adams was living the life of her dreams. She was a happy, vivacious mother of two who had married her high school sweetheart right out of college. For almost 20 years, Gary had been a very devoted husband and loving father.

Katie was employed as a supervisor in the Human Resources Department at MedSol, a large pharmaceutical company located in the northern suburbs of Chicago. Her future at the company looked bright. The human resources director had told her that if she continued to develop at her current rate, a promotion to a first-level manager position was just around the corner.

Then one day, everything changed. Katie decided to work at home that day, so she was sitting at the family-room computer when Gary came through the front door shortly after lunch.

"Why are you home so early?" Katie asked. "Is something wrong?"

What followed was the conversation no wife or husband ever wants to have: Gary was leaving—with no warning, no real explanation, just some vague claim that he needed some time to decide if he wanted to stay married. Within minutes, he was out the door, suitcase in hand, his new phone number on a Post-it stuck on the refrigerator.

Katie decided to take the high road and protect her children from the knock-down, drag-out fight of a bitterly contested divorce. She remained civil throughout the proceedings and wound up with custody of the children, the house, a car, some cash, and what she considered to be a reasonable monthly child support payment.

Several weeks later, the child support payment failed to arrive. After a few calls, Katie discovered that Gary had been fired from his job and moved to Italy to the hometown of his new wife—Angela Conti, a woman whom Katie had known for years!

This further shock, this further betrayal, and the realization that there would be no more child support were enough to push Katie over the edge. After she hung up the phone, she cried for a few minutes, feeling sorry for herself. Then she got angry—extremely angry. And she stayed that way.

REVVED!

From Bad to Worse

As time passed, Katie's devastation began to take its toll. Wary of being hurt again, the previously trusting and outgoing Katie began to distance herself from her friends and coworkers. During the next year, she increasingly took her anger out on those around her—especially at work.

Katie did something many people do—she let her personal life sabotage her career.

When the people she supervised made mistakes, she lashed out at them. When her staff had deadlines or assignments, she looked over their shoulders and micromanaged them to death. She said she was too busy for the friendly exchanges she now referred to as "idle chatter." Katie Adams, once the ultimate people person, was developing both distrust and contempt for nearly everyone.

Katie's defensiveness had a disastrous impact on her effectiveness as a supervisor. Department morale and productivity plunged dramatically, and many members of her staff were trying to transfer out of her unit.

The final blow came one Friday afternoon in January, when Katie learned that the promotion she had been promised was going to someone who reported to her: Sean McCarthy, who had once been Katie's friend, but who now struck her as a very divisive and self-centered person. He and Katie no longer got along at all—and now he was going to be her boss!

[3]

Katie was livid, and she immediately set out to find Jackie Peters, the director of human resources, and demand an explanation. "You promised that promotion to me!" she cried.

"You're absolutely right, Katie," Jackie replied. "I did promise you that promotion—*if* you continued to progress in your development.

"But then you changed, and the performance of your entire department went south. Do you realize that a year ago, you were the highest-ranked supervisor in Human Resources, and now you are the lowest? Nobody likes working for you any more. People in your department have started calling you the 'Witch on Steroids.' Is something going on in . . . ?"

"My personal life is none of your business!" Katie snapped.

"You're right," said Jackie, "but the way you just assumed I was going to ask you a personal question is a prime example of how much you have changed. You appear to be angry all the time. Taking that anger out on the people you work with is a guaranteed formula for failure."

"We all want the old Katie Adams back. But if you can't get your act back together in pretty short order, I'll have no choice but to take away your supervisory responsibilities. Why don't you use some vacation time, take next week off, and see if you can't work through your situation."

REVVED!

NICE MANAGERS GET RESULTS

Some years back, a group of researchers studied 16,000 corporate managers. The results surprised many skeptics. They showed that the highest achievers were those who valued people as highly as they valued profits.

Katie realized how much she'd like to have the old Katie Adams back as well. "Thanks," she replied. "I think I'll take you up on your offer."

TWO!

KATIE SPENT THE WEEKEND ALONE—the kids were in Wisconsin with the high school ski club. On Saturday, she took a long walk to try to clear her head. At one point, while she was waiting at a crosswalk, her eye was drawn to a huge poster on the side of a city bus idling next to her. In the center of the ad was the photograph of an early-middle-aged man, flanked on either side by two statements: "Ask Dr. Allen" and "He has all the answers."

What a joke, thought Katie. *I used to think I had all the answers.*

Searching for Answers

Thinking about how to change her work situation turned out to be fruitless. So when Sunday afternoon rolled around and she hadn't made any progress, Katie concluded that she needed some extra help. Her friend Jennifer Johnson was a career coach, but Katie had never sought her professional advice. Given the circumstances, Katie decided it was time to give Jennifer a call.

"Hello, Jen, this is Katie. I hate to impose, but I'm having some problems at work. I was hoping you could help."

"What's going on?" asked Jennifer.

Katie filled Jennifer in on the lost promotion, her new boss, and what Jackie Peters had said about her possible demotion. She even told Jennifer about her new, wretched nickname.

"Witch on Steroids"? gasped Jennifer. "That doesn't sound like you. Did she tell you why they feel this way?"

"They think I'm negative, unapproachable, and hypercritical—and those are her exact words. She thinks it's because I'm angry and I'm taking my anger out on the people I supervise."

Jennifer thought for a moment before responding in a tone that was both gentle and firm. "If you ask me, I do think you are still hurting over your divorce," she said. "And you're worried about being hurt again."

Katie started to cry. "You're right," she sobbed. "I have nightmares about being hurt again. Aside from you and my kids, I'm not sure I'll ever be able to trust anyone again."

"Katie, you have to let go of the past and get on with your life. What happened between you, Gary, and Angela was terrible, but the chances of your getting hurt like that again are slim at best. What you need to do is to let go of your anger and start letting people back into your life. If you expect people to work hard for you again, you're going to have to reach out and truly care about them. Because, when you do, they will care about you in return—that's the way life works."

"That's easy for you to say," said Katie. "I've thought about this a lot. I've tried to open up and trust people again, but each time I try, I break out in a sweat. I'm just not ready yet. There must be a way to work effectively with people that doesn't require me to take that risk again."

"You mean a system for getting others to do what you want that doesn't require any emotional involvement?"

"That's exactly it!" exclaimed Katie.

"I'm not sure if that actually exists," said Jennifer. "But at least now I know what you are looking for. Give me a couple of days to see if I can find something that will help you. In the meantime, I want you to totally block your work situation out of your mind. Take some time for yourself and relax."

Control Your Emotions

The next day, Jennifer called an old friend from graduate school, Michael Allen, a psychologist and the host of a popular radio talk show. She told him all about Katie, her bitter divorce, and her current difficulties at work.

"Without realizing it," said Michael, "what your friend is asking for is a set of tools that will allow her to influence the people she works with in a positive way, even though the pain she is feeling inside is anything but positive."

"Yes, that's exactly right," declared Jennifer. "But that sounds like an awfully difficult thing to pull off," she added.

"I won't lie to you, Jen; it isn't easy, but I have seen it work in a great many situations," shot back Michael. "Katie has to somehow condition herself to act in a way she does not feel."

"That sounds . . . well, a bit insincere, don't you think, Michael?"

"Let me tell you a story, Katie. When I was going through my master's degree program, I had the toughest time getting motivated. I was in the midst of a messy breakup with my girlfriend of four years, and the workload was killing me. I thought I would have to drop out of the program."

"You never told me about this, Michael. Why not? I might have been able to at least provide moral support."

"I know, but I withdrew from everyone. I figured there was little hope of turning things around until one of my professors gave me a book that changed my perspective. I don't remember the title, but the author was the famous motivation expert Og Mandino. In the book, there is a passage that I have committed to memory and recited to myself hundreds of times since then. It goes like this:

Weak is he who allows his emotions to control his actions. Strong is he who allows his actions to control his emotions.

"What exactly does that mean, and how does it apply to Katie?" asked Jennifer.

"It's pretty simple," explained Michael. "If she really is so scarred inside, then her only remaining option is to reach down within herself and force herself to change her behavior."

"You mean, act as if she really cared about her colleagues, even if she may not feel it?" Jennifer asked skeptically.

"That's pretty much it," Michael explained. "To get the old Katie back, she needs to behave in a way that is consistent with the person she once was, regardless of how she feels. The keys to making this work are patience and a little discipline."

REVVED!

Today I Will Be Master of My Emotions

Og Mandino

Today I will be master of my emotions.

The tides advance; the tides recede. Winter goes and summer
comes. Summer wanes and the cold increases.

The sun rises; the sun sets. . . .

All nature is a circle of moods and I am a part of nature and so,
like the tides, my moods will rise; my moods will fall.

It is one of nature's tricks, little understood, that each day I
awaken with moods that have changed from yesterday.

Yesterday's joy will become tomorrow's sadness; yet today's
sadness will grow into tomorrow's joy.

Inside me is a wheel, constantly turning from sadness to joy,
from exultation to depression, from happiness to melancholy . . . .

Today I will be master of my emotions.

REVVED!

In Search of the "Old" Katie

"So how do we start?" asked Jennifer. "Before her husband left her, Katie was the kind of person that everyone loved. I know that person is still inside her, because she is still the same old Katie around me."

"I think I know what we need to do," said Michael. "Several years ago I introduced a new program that many of my listeners have embraced with great success. It's called *Looking Out for Number Two*.

"It involves opening up and truly caring about those around you, knowing that they're going to care back. The goal of the program is to build your own personal army of advocates—a group of people who absolutely can't do enough for you. When you think about it, that's really what being a successful supervisor is all about."

"Sounds perfect," said Jennifer, "but I doubt that we'll get her to buy into the caring that's required. She's just too afraid of being hurt again."

Michael looked away for a few seconds, deep in thought, then suddenly perked up. "I think I've got it! If Katie is too hurt and too scared to risk trying to care about those around her, why don't we tell her that she only needs to pretend the caring that's required—role-play it, if you will."

Jennifer frowned. "You mean trick her?"

"We're just helping her get out of her own way," said Michael. "My job will be to convince her that she can treat her staff and coworkers as if she cared without actually having to feel that way."

"I get it," said Jennifer. "She'll think she's keeping everybody at a safe distance by pretending. And once Katie starts acting like someone who cares, people are going to start caring about her in return. It will be only a matter of time before the old Katie returns."

"And that's when we tell her that she's been caring all along," said Michael.

"What's step 1? Do you want to see her in person?"

"Well," replied Michael, "it sounds like Katie wants to keep everyone at arm's length, so have her call me after my show on Friday. Tell her to identify herself as 'Katie from Deerfield.' Also, suggest that she listen to an hour or so of my show to get a feel for where I'm coming from. And don't let on that you've shared so much of her personal history with me—I think it might make her more defensive."

"Thanks. This is exciting. Now I'm really looking forward to my meeting with Katie tomorrow. I want you to know that this is a very kind thing you are doing for a very nice person."

Michael smiled and said, "That's what friends are for."

REVVED!

MASTER YOUR EMOTIONS

Even the best leaders have personal problems at one time or another. In those situations, the most effective leaders reach down inside themselves to find the strength to keep their emotions in check, especially at work.

Putting the Plan in Motion

Despite Jennifer's advice that she relax, Katie spent the first part of the week on pins and needles, wondering what Jennifer would tell her. Finally, Katie was at Jennifer's office, where she found Jennifer standing in the doorway, waiting to greet her with a hug.

"Come on in and sit down," said Jennifer.

"I can't tell you how excited I am to hear what you have to say," Katie said.

"Well," said Jennifer, "I have some good news and some bad news. Which would you like to hear first?"

"Why don't you give me the bad news first? I've gotten pretty used to hearing that recently," said Katie, her excitement waning.

"Okay," said Jennifer. "The bad news is that I personally can't help you. Everything I have in my career-coaching bag of tricks requires you to open up and care about the people who stand between you and success. That's not what you're looking for." As Jennifer looked over at Katie, it was obvious that she was disappointed.

"All right," said Katie, "now tell me the good news."

"The good news," continued Jennifer, "is that while I personally can't help you, I think I have found someone who can."

Katie sat up straight and breathed a sigh of relief. "Tell me, who is this person?"

"His name is Michael Allen, and he hosts a career/self-improvement talk show on WGO radio every weekday afternoon from three until six called *Ask Dr. Allen*. Have you ever heard of him?"

Katie thought for a moment. "Dr. Allen . . . isn't he that pop psychologist whose picture is plastered on the side of nearly every bus in Chicago?"

"That's the guy," replied Jennifer with a chuckle.

"And you know him?"

"Yes, he and I went to grad school together."

"Wow!" said Katie, "I'm impressed. Why do you think he can help?"

"Because he has a program that is tailor-made for people like you who want to stay emotionally detached. He would like you to call him after the show on Friday. Just tell him that you're Katie from Deerfield, and Dr. Allen will take it from there. He also suggested that you listen to part of his show before you call."

"Wouldn't it make more sense if I made an appointment to see him in person?" asked Katie.

"I asked that, too," replied Jennifer, "but he said that if you're looking to limit your personal involvement, then the phone call format is perfect for you."

"You're right," said Katie, "but I must admit that I'm a little nervous."

"Don't worry; Dr. Allen is a kind and wonderful person. You'll be fine," said Jennifer, handing Katie one of Dr. Allen's business cards.

"I can't thank you enough for helping," said Katie as she gave Jennifer a good-bye hug.

"I'm only too happy to help," said Jennifer. "Besides, that's what friends are for."

THREE!

AT 5:00 ON FRIDAY AFTERNOON, Katie tuned her radio to station WGO. After a few minutes of news, weather, and traffic reports and a few commercials, she heard a smooth, pleasant male voice.

"Hello Chicagoland! Welcome back to the *Ask Dr. Allen* show. I see we have Margo from Park Ridge on the line. Welcome, Margo."

"Hi, Dr. Allen. I'm a long-time listener and first-time caller, and I want you to know that it's a thrill to be on your show."

"My pleasure, Margo. What can I do for you?"

"I'm calling about my neighbor. The kids in the neighborhood happily pick her dandelions without her having to ask. Her newspaper is always on her stoop, while I have to retrieve mine from the hedge. If she's not home, the mailman always drops her packages with me or another neighbor, but if I'm not home, I get a notice to go to the post office. How can I get these people to treat me like they do her?"

"Excellent question, Margo. It sounds like your neighbor has what we here on *Ask Dr. Allen* call 'Personality Plus.' Contrary to popular belief, Personality Plus is not something you're born with—it's something you develop by being nice to people and making them feel special. I'll bet your neighbor is able to greet all the children in the neighborhood by their names and has taken the time to get to know the newspaper delivery person and the mail person. Take the time to do the same, and watch how your life quickly changes for the better."

"That's a great answer. Thanks, Dr. Allen."

"Next, we have Bill on the line from Joliet. Welcome, Bill. How can I help you?"

"I want to start my own business, but almost all my friends and coworkers are telling me to stay where I am because they say there is a strong possibility that I might fail. What should I do?"

"First, let me offer you a little insight into why your friends and coworkers are discouraging you. You see, many people secretly harbor the notion of one day starting their own business, but few want to risk doing it. When you admit that you have the courage to at least give it a try, you become a threat to them. If you succeed, you'll make them look bad. In addition, they interpret your desire to follow your dream as a negative judgment about what they are doing. So, their natural response is going to be negative and critical."

"Thanks for the insight, Dr. Allen, but you still haven't answered my question."

"Perhaps a quote from Theodore Roosevelt will help. It goes like this:

> Far better is it to dare mighty things than to take rank with those poor spirits who neither enjoy much nor suffer much, because they live in the gray twilight that knows not victory nor defeat.

"I say ignore your friends and coworkers and go for it, Bill!"

"Thanks, Dr. Allen. That's what I needed to hear."

"You're welcome, Bill, and all the best to you and your new venture."

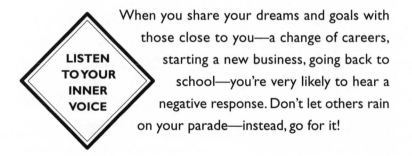

LISTEN TO YOUR INNER VOICE

When you share your dreams and goals with those close to you—a change of careers, starting a new business, going back to school—you're very likely to hear a negative response. Don't let others rain on your parade—instead, go for it!

REVVED!

A Ray of Hope

Katie was impressed. Clearly, there was a lot more depth to Dr. Allen than she had initially given him credit for.

"Our next caller is Scott, calling from downtown. Welcome, Scott. How can I help you?"

"You already have, Dr. Allen, and I'm just calling to say thank you."

"You're welcome," he replied with a chuckle. "Tell me more."

"I'm one of the Realtors who attended your program at the real estate convention a few months ago. I listened carefully when you said we should pay special attention to our old customers and not ignore them after we've made the sale. When I got back to my office, I started calling my old customers—not to try to sell them anything, just to say hello and ask how they were doing. As a result, my phone has been ringing nonstop with people who want me to list their homes for them. I can't thank you enough."

"Scott, you have made my day! Keep up the good work."

Before Katie knew it, the show was over and it was time for her to call Dr. Allen. The phone rang twice before she heard, "This is Dr. Allen."

"This is Katie from Deerfield."

"Hi, Katie! I've been expecting your call. How may I help you?"

"To make a long story short, I am in deep trouble at work and could even lose my job unless I can turn things around in short order."

"That sounds awful. What happened?"

Katie began to tell Dr. Allen her story, surprised at how comfortable he made her feel. By the time she got to the part about talking to Jennifer, she had forgotten that she was talking to a celebrity. "Our mutual friend, Jennifer, told me you have a program that makes it possible for people like me to be effective in working with people while keeping them at a safe distance, to minimize the risk of being hurt."

"I do have such a program," said Dr. Allen. "And once you learn it, you will be able to get others to work hard for you—and still stay at a safe distance. In other words, you'll be able to turn things around without having to become emotionally involved."

Become Master of Yourself

"That sounds great. Is your program easy to use?"

"You bet, but it does require a little acting," Dr. Allen replied.

"Why is that?" Katie asked.

"Because caring is absolutely necessary when it comes to getting others excited about doing things on your behalf—that's what a supervisor's job is all about. Since you are unable to care about the people you work with, you're going to have to, well . . . for lack of a better phrase, role-play the caring part—that's where the acting comes in."

"I'm not sure I follow," said Katie.

"Let me put it this way: even though you are not able to care about the people you work with, if you expect them to bust their tails on your behalf, they have to *think* you do. In other words, you have to go through the motions of caring in a very convincing manner."

"Now I get it. But I must confess, it all sounds a bit . . . well, insincere, don't you think, Doctor?"

"Let me ask you this," said Dr. Allen. "Would you put yourself out for someone who you thought didn't care about you and was only out to exploit you?"

"No way!"

"Neither would anyone else," said Dr. Allen. "That's why you have to at the very least *play the part* of the caring supervisor in order to become a successful supervisor once again. One of the keys to the program is a simple but powerful mantra, one I learned from one of the great experts on motivation:

Today I will be master of my emotions.

"Well, I've got nothing to lose, so I will give it my best shot."

"Great, Katie. You won't be sorry."

FOUR!

"FIRST, KATIE, let me congratulate you for having the courage to try my program."

"It's not like I have a whole lot of choice, Doctor. If I don't do something to turn around my situation at work, I'm going to lose my job—I'm desperate!"

"Maybe that's good," said Dr. Allen. "One thing I've observed over the years is that desperate pupils make the best learners."

Take Baby Steps

"My program has only three simple steps. The first step is called *Winning Them Over.*"

"What does Winning Them Over involve?" asked Katie.

"It's just like it sounds," said Dr. Allen. "As it stands now, the people you work with consider you their enemy, and your behavior toward them reinforces this belief. The goal of the Winning Them Over step of my program is to turn these same people into enduring allies who are eager to support you in your role as supervisor. What I'm going to give you now is a game plan that will enable you to jump-start that process."

"Great! At this point, I'm ready to try anything."

"Good," said Dr. Allen. "Here's what I want you to do: Monday morning, as you pull into the parking lot at work, I want you to plaster a smile on your face that makes you look like one of the happiest people in the world."

"But, Doctor—that hardly sounds like a solution to anything," shot back Katie. "And it's been a long time since I felt like smiling."

"Patience, Katie, please. It doesn't matter if you're not happy. Remember the mantra: 'Today I become master of my emotions.' I also want you to greet every person you come into contact with cheerfully and find something nice to say to them."

"Like what?" asked Katie.

"Little things like, 'Good morning,' or, 'How are you today?' or, 'You look very nice today,'" said Dr. Allen. "Also, keep in mind, the people you work with are not used to seeing you behave in this manner, so expect a few puzzled looks, rolled eyes, and even snide comments behind your back. Don't let this bother you. All it means is that you caught them off guard. Once they get used to the new you, these behaviors will stop. It's a normal part of the process of Winning Them Over."

"That's going to be a challenge, because I'm not comfortable behaving like that now. In fact, Doctor, the whole thing sounds, well contrived . . . or, at the very least, it seems like a simplistic response to a serious problem," replied Katie dejectedly.

"Maybe so, Katie, but for now, at least, would you let *me* play the part of doctor?"

That at least got Katie to smile, something she had done very little of lately, she thought.

"Look, I know it sounds simplistic, and I also know it's going to be hard for you to do this initially," responded Dr. Allen, "but I think you are going to be pleasantly surprised by the results."

"Is there anything else I need to do?" Katie asked.

"There are two more things I'll want you to do, but I want you to wait until Wednesday before you start to do them."

"Why is that?" asked Katie.

"Because, just by smiling and saying something positive, you're already going to shock the people you work with. Doing everything associated with Winning Them Over right away is too much to handle—both for them and for you. So, I think it's best if we break this first step of my program into two baby steps. By Wednesday, some of the shock will have worn off, and they will be better able to handle more of the 'new Katie.'"

"What else do I need to do?"

"On Wednesday, as well as smiling and saying something positive when you greet people, I want you to actively engage your colleagues. For example, ask them how things are going. And when they answer, I want you to stop what you're doing and actively listen to what they have to say."

"What do you mean by 'actively listen'?" asked Katie.

"I want you to focus solely on what these people have to say and nothing else—no looking at your watch, reading your e-mail, or any other form of multitasking while they're talking to you. Ask a few questions about what they're saying. And do the same thing when people come to you with a question or a problem."

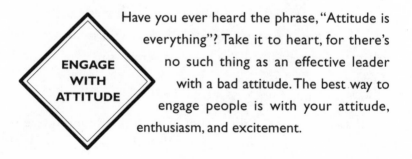

Have you ever heard the phrase, "Attitude is everything"? Take it to heart, for there's no such thing as an effective leader with a bad attitude. The best way to engage people is with your attitude, enthusiasm, and excitement.

ENGAGE WITH ATTITUDE

"Let me see if I get it," said Katie. "The best way for me to engage people is to send the clear message that I am interested in them. This is the message they need to hear loud and clear before they will even consider doing those things that will make me a successful supervisor once again."

"You've got it, Katie," chuckled Dr. Allen. "But let me warn you, this is where the 'mastering my emotions' part can become somewhat challenging."

"Why is that?" asked Katie.

"Because some people are going to share things with you that you haven't the slightest interest in. While you're listening, you'll be saying to yourself, 'I'd rather be anyplace but here' or 'When is this ever going to end?' You'll want to yawn or look off into space rather than look at the person who is talking.

"However, if you want to turn your situation around and be in line for a promotion once again, you're going to have to buck up and act in a manner that convinces these people that you really are interested in what they're saying."

"I'll give it the old college try," said Katie. "I have nothing to lose and everything to gain."

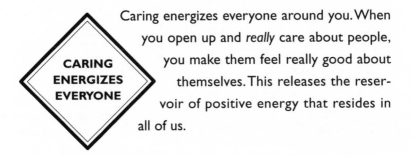

CARING ENERGIZES EVERYONE

Caring energizes everyone around you. When you open up and *really* care about people, you make them feel really good about themselves. This releases the reservoir of positive energy that resides in all of us.

REVVED!

"I like your attitude," said Dr. Allen. "Call me any time before or after the show if you have any problems. And, I want you to call me next Friday to bring me up to date on your progress."

"Will do," said Katie. "I'll talk to you then."

FIVE!

KATIE PULLED INTO THE MEDSOL PARKING LOT
Monday morning after a weekend spent developing the
smile that Dr. Allen had told her she would need. She
found that smiling was much easier if she focused on something that brought joy and happiness into her life, like her
children.

So as she got out of her car, she thought about the portrait of her children displayed on her mantel. Almost like
magic, a smile appeared on her face. Katie had also devel-
oped a list of positive things to say so that she wouldn't be
at a loss for words when she greeted people. As she walked
toward the building entrance, she was suddenly eager to see
how well the good doctor's program would work.

REVVED!

It's Working

As Katie came through the door, the first person she saw was Joe, at the security desk. "Good morning, Joe," she said cheerfully as she showed him her badge. "You certainly look happy this morning!"

Joe appeared somewhat stunned before he replied, "Good morning, Ms. Adams. To tell you the truth, I am. I started working out at the gym a few weeks ago, and it's changed my whole outlook on things."

"That's wonderful, Joe. Keep up the good work!"

"I will, Ms. Adams, and you have a nice day."

"Thank you," she said as she walked through the security door that led to her department. She couldn't help but notice that it was the first time in ages that Joe had told her to have a nice day.

The next person that Katie saw was Alicia, her administrative assistant. "Good morning, Alicia," she said as she smiled. "Great shoes!"

Katie could see that the compliment took Alicia by surprise. "Pardon me?" she responded with a perplexed look on her face.

"Oh," said Katie, "I just said I like your shoes."

"Thanks, Ms. Adams. I got them on sale! By the way, Mr. McCarthy stopped by a few minutes ago. He wants to see you in his office right away."

"Thank you, Alicia."

On her way to Sean McCarthy's office, she noticed Greg and Justin, both employment specialists, coming down the hallway toward her. It immediately became apparent to Katie that they were trying to avoid eye contact with her. "Good morning, Greg. Good morning, Justin," she said in an upbeat voice as she smiled at them. "Have a nice day."

"You too, Ms. Adams," the two men said in unison as they walked by her.

Moments later, she could overhear one of them ask the other, "What's up with the witch?"

Remembering that Dr. Allen had warned her about this type of reaction softened the sting of the remark, but she found it hard to stay positive as she approached Sean's office. The thought of him being her boss was more than her "mastering my emotions" mantra could endure. *I'll just bet he wants to see me,* she thought. *Mr. McCarthy? Come on! Who is he trying to fool?*

Putting the Program to the Test

Sean was waiting for Katie when she arrived. "Katie, I have no choice but to put you officially on notice," he said in a condescending tone of voice. "You have two months to turn your performance around as a supervisor, or you're out of here. Any questions?"

"Thank you for sugar-coating things for me," she said.

"I believe in being up front," he said with his arms folded across his chest.

Katie restrained herself from saying anything that would make things worse, but glared at him nonetheless. "All I ask is that you give me the full two months," she finally said.

"You've got two months and nothing more," he said as he walked toward his desk.

"Why, thank you, Sean. Your generosity overwhelms me."

As she walked back to her office, she realized that Dr. Allen wouldn't have approved of the way she had handled that situation and that she had let her disdain for Sean take her out of her game plan. She vowed to get a grip.

After settling in her office for a while, Katie regained her composure enough to visit Sheila Davis, who was working on a salary comparison report for her. Sheila and Katie were not on particularly friendly terms and had even clashed on numerous occasions. On her way to Sheila's work area in the accounting department, Katie reflected that this encounter would really put Dr. Allen's program to the test.

Once again, Katie thought about the portrait of her children in order to make sure that her smile was convincing. "Good morning, Sheila. I hope you're having one so far."

Sheila replied in a hostile tone of voice, "If you're looking for that salary comparison report, it won't be done until Thursday, the date that you said you needed it by. If you're here to bug me about getting it done earlier, I'll save you the time . . . it will be ready on Thursday!"

Katie struggled for a few seconds to find something positive to say. "Sheila, I know you'll have the report done on time—you always do, and that's why I'm here. On my way to work this morning, I was doing some thinking, and I realized that it had been a long time since I said 'thank you' for all the great work you have done for me during my time here at MedSol."

"Long time—how about never!" exclaimed Sheila in a sarcastic tone of voice. "I didn't think you even noticed that I stayed late to get reports done for you."

"I'm sorry, Sheila; it was wrong to take you for granted. I want you to know that those days are over, and I promise that I'll never take you for granted again."

"Pardon me if I sit down," said Sheila, "but I never thought I'd see the day when you would go out of your way to apologize. I really appreciate it, and I'm sorry that I was so rude to you just now."

"That's okay, Sheila. If I were in your shoes, I don't think I would have been any nicer. I hope you have a great day," said Katie, as she got ready to leave.

"You have a great day, too," replied Sheila with a smile. "And if things work out the way I expect them to, I just might be able to get your report done by Wednesday."

"That would be great," said Katie as she started toward her office, "but there's no need to stress yourself out. Take care."

"You, too."

As she walked back to her office, Katie had to admit that Dr. Allen deserved credit on at least one count: he had said that she would see instant results from using his program, and he was right! Katie was suddenly eager to see how the rest of the week would unfold.

Katie's entire day was filled with similar episodes. Driving home, she was struck by how many times she had heard the phrase, "Have a nice day." She took that as a sign that the "mastering my emotions" part of the program was working.

The next morning, the security guard greeted her with a big smile. "Good morning, Ms. Adams."

"Good morning, Joe."

"Guess what, Ms. Adams? I weighed in at my health club last night, and so far, I've lost 15 pounds. I can't begin to tell you how great I feel."

"Why, that's wonderful!" exclaimed Katie. "Keep up the good work, Joe and have a nice day."

"You do the same, Ms. Adams."

THE POWER OF POSITIVE ACTION

Don't be nice to people just because you want something from them. Be positive just to be positive, and watch how your life changes for the better.

REVVED!

On the way to work on Wednesday, Katie reminded herself that she was supposed to start asking people about what was going on in their lives and actively listening to their answers. She had spent part of the last two evenings jotting down a number of different ways of asking this, so she was ready.

As she pulled into the MedSol parking lot, Katie went through what was quickly becoming part of her daily routine—she focused on the portrait of her children to bring a smile to her face.

As she walked through the door, Joe greeted her and then said, "Ms. Adams, do you have a minute?"

Katie was well rehearsed and ready with her response. "Sure, Joe, I always have time for you. What's up?"

"I just got the pictures back from my daughter's basketball tournament last weekend, and I thought you might like to see them."

He has got to be kidding, Katie thought, before remembering Dr. Allen's program. "I'd love to."

Joe got up from behind his desk with what must have been at least 30 photographs and began to explain them to Katie one at a time.

As she offered a comment or question about each of the pictures, she remembered that Dr. Allen had said that this would be challenging. He was right—she thought that stack of pictures would never end!

REVVED!

"You must be very proud of your daughter," Katie said, after looking at the last photograph.

"You bet I am," he said as he went back to his desk. "Have a nice day, Ms. Adams."

"You too, Joe," said Katie, heading toward her office for what she feared might be a long day.

As Katie walked into her office, she noticed Sheila's salary comparison report sitting her desk. Attached was a note that read,

> Katie:
> I know how eager you are to get this report, so I finished it before I went home last night. Have a great day!
>
> Sheila

Once again, Katie was amazed at how well the program was working—even though she was still only on step 1. Remembering that she had told Sheila that she would never take her for granted again, she turned her mind to doing something to show her appreciation.

She opted to do it by e-mail:

> Dear Sheila,
> It was so wonderful to find that salary comparison report on my desk when I arrived this morning. I

can't begin to tell you how much I appreciate all the extra effort you went to in order to finish the report a day early. Let me put it this way, you made my day!

Gratefully,
Katie

For the rest of Wednesday and Thursday, Katie continued greeting everyone by name, saying something positive, and asking how things were going in their lives. As instructed, she listened to their answers with what looked like strong interest. She did the same thing for people who came to her with questions or problems.

Taking Note of the Changes

Driving to work on Friday, Katie remembered that she was supposed to call Dr. Allen to give a progress report that afternoon. She had been so busy putting the program to work, she realized, that she hadn't taken the time to see if any overall changes had taken hold. She made a mental note to do so as she pulled into the parking lot.

Once again, she remembered the portrait of her children as she got out of her car and walked through the entrance of her building with a smile on her face. The first sign that changes were starting to take hold came from Joe, who greeted her with an enthusiastic, "Good morning, Katie," instead of "Good morning, Ms. Adams." As Katie walked by his desk, Joe handed her a small vase containing an orchid that he had grown in his basement.

"How sweet," said Katie, who by now had the "mastering her emotions" mantra down pretty well. "It's beautiful," she continued. "Thank you so much."

"You've been so nice to me this week, I felt like doing something nice for you in return. Have a great day."

"You, too, Joe, and thanks again for your thoughtfulness," she said as an inexplicable lump appeared in her throat.

Shortly after she reached her office, Greg and Justin showed up. On Monday they had tried to avoid eye contact with Katie, but today they were all smiles, eager to discuss a way of reorganizing some of the department's work to improve its overall productivity. Katie listened intently, asking a few questions and offering minor suggestions that Greg and Justin enthusiastically welcomed.

"Well, what do you think?" they asked, waiting for Katie's response.

Katie knew that if their idea really worked, it could go a long way toward eliminating her department's backlog and getting her out of the doghouse, so she didn't want to dampen their enthusiasm. She looked at the two men, paused for a few seconds, and said, "Go for it, guys! You have my full support."

The two men left Katie's office higher than a kite with enthusiasm. She had never seen those two guys that excited about working on a project before. She decided that she must have said the right thing. "This is starting to feel really good," she thought.

SINCERE APPRECIATION GETS RESULTS

One of the deepest needs of our human existence is the need to be appreciated. Each and every one of us absolutely loves to be appreciated for who we are and what we do.

It was 2:00, and Katie decided that it was a good time to call Dr. Allen. Before she went to her office, she toured her department to see if any changes had taken place since Monday. The first thing that struck her was that everyone was working like beavers, and that nearly everyone was smiling.

A week ago, nearly everyone had been wearing a frown or a scowl, spending too much time whispering or complaining in small groups. *What a switch,* she thought. Her next observation told the tale. As she walked through her department, people no longer ran for cover or tried to avoid contact with her. Instead, she heard an enthusiastic, "Hi,

REVVED!

Katie!" as she approached each one, and a pleasant, "Have a nice day," as she left his or her company.

Based on what she'd seen so far, Katie had to conclude that Dr. Allen's program was working, and she was looking forward to talking to him.

SIX!

WHEN SHE GOT BACK TO HER OFFICE, Katie closed the door and called Dr. Allen. "Hi, this is Katie from Deerfield."

"Tell me, Katie, did you have a good week?"

"I sure did. I'm actually starting to think that I've got the Winning Them Over step pretty well down."

"What do you think about my program so far?" asked Dr. Allen.

"I can't believe how well it is working. I mean, people from other departments who didn't like me at all are now giving me gifts, sending me thank-you notes, and giving my projects their top priority—I can't get over the transformation."

"How about the people in your department?" asked Dr. Allen.

"Morale is definitely up, and so is productivity."

"How can you tell?" asked Dr. Allen.

"Everyone is smiling. On top of that, they're working hard and making suggestions on how to improve things."

"Have you noticed any difference in how they respond to you?"

"That's probably the most noticeable change. Instead of running the other way when they see me coming, they actually seem like they are glad to see me. They're always telling me to have a nice day. And it sounds like they even mean it."

"How does all this make you feel?"

"That's the interesting part. I haven't felt this good in a long time. I'm actually starting to enjoy coming to work again."

"Well done, Katie!" said Dr. Allen. "It sounds like you're back in the driver's seat."

The Second Step

"Things are definitely getting better," said Katie. "I think I am ready to take this to the next level. Where do we go from here?"

"The second step," said Dr. Allen, "is called *Blowing Them Away*."

"What does that mean?" Katie asked.

"The people you work with are getting the message that you care about them. They are starting to trust you and are excited about working hard for you, which is necessary if you want to become a successful supervisor again.

"The goal of the *Blowing Them Away* step is to take that excitement to the next level. Once you get this step down, the job of supervisor becomes a matter of sitting back and enjoying the ride."

"This step sounds fascinating; what's it about?" asked Katie.

"It involves singling out people who have just gone the extra mile for you and then Blowing Them Away with the way you express your appreciation. You have to do it in a way that makes these people feel so great that they can't wait to do it again."

"Can you give me an example?" asked Katie.

"Let me ask you this," said Dr. Allen. "Did any of the people you work with go the extra mile for you this past week?"

"Absolutely! Sheila in accounting worked late to finish a report I was waiting for a day early."

"Excellent! And how did you thank her?"

"I sent her an e-mail telling how much I appreciated the extra effort. Also, I told her that she had made my day, and I closed the e-mail with 'gratefully.'"

"Katie, let me say this," said Dr. Allen. "You did what most people would consider the right and proper thing to do. But, if you want Sheila to get excited about staying late to get your reports done early again, what you've done to thank her is not enough."

"What do you mean?" asked Katie.

"By sending Sheila your e-mail, you singled her out for going the extra mile, but you didn't Blow Her Away with your expression of appreciation."

"Why is that so important?"

"Because going the extra mile usually involves lots of extra effort and inconvenience that's not required by a person's job description. Sheila didn't get paid to stay late at work to finish your report a day early; she did it as a *special* favor for you."

"I see your point," said Katie. "If I don't make her feel special in return, she will think that she put in all that effort for nothing, and that I'm taking her for granted again."

"That's right," said Dr. Allen, "and she will be less inclined to do special favors for you in the future."

"What should I have done?"

"Instead of just sending her the thank-you note, you should have sent a note to her boss telling him what a wonderful employee Sheila is, what she did that deserves his attention, and how fortunate he is to have her working for him. Besides sending this note to Sheila's boss, see to it that Sheila, her boss's boss, and the president of your company also get copies. And by all means, do not send this note by e-mail."

"Why not?"

"Because e-mail is too impersonal and too easily deleted to have the impact needed to blow someone away. Everyone should get a hard copy. Now let me ask you this: how do you think Sheila is going to respond when she gets her copy of that note?"

"She is going to be totally Blown Away," Katie laughed.

"That's exactly right!" exclaimed Dr. Allen. "And when she finishes reading the letter and sees who else received copies, she is going to find an excuse to come over to your office. And guess what she is going to say?"

"I'm not really sure."

"She's going to utter those magical words that tell you that the Blowing Them Away step of my program is working."

"What are they?" asked Katie.

"Is there anything else I can do for you?"

"Why are they the magical words?" asked Katie.

"Good question," said Dr. Allen. "When you blow someone away, you make him or her feel absolutely great—a feeling everyone wants to experience again and again. Since going the extra mile for you is what led to these great feelings in the first place, this person now thinks that doing it again will give her the chance to feel great all over again."

"So, this person starts to eagerly search for *other* opportunities to go the extra mile for me," said Katie. "I think I am starting to see the light."

"Exactly!" said Dr. Allen. "And as long as you don't disappoint them with your expressions of appreciation when they do, their behavior will continue. But hold on, Katie, this is only the tip of the iceberg! There's much more to this part, and I think you're going to like it."

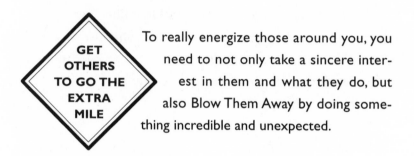

GET OTHERS TO GO THE EXTRA MILE

To really energize those around you, you need to not only take a sincere interest in them and what they do, but also Blow Them Away by doing something incredible and unexpected.

The Multiplier Effect

"Blowing Them Away also has a huge bonus associated with it. I refer to this bonus as the *Multiplier Effect*."

"What's that?" asked Katie.

"When you blow someone away with your expression of appreciation, you almost always make that person's day. As a result, he or she is not only happy, but excited as well. When people are both happy and excited, they can't help but tell others what made them feel that way.

"These people, in turn, tell more people, and the word about you spreads quickly. All of a sudden you have lots and lots of people, many of whom you may have never interacted with, also looking for opportunities to go the extra mile for you."

"What I hear you saying is that I'll start to build a large group of people who absolutely can't do enough for me."

"Exactly! I refer to this as your *personal army of advocates*. Let me tell you, when this army starts to fall into place, being a successful supervisor, or anything else for that matter, becomes a piece of cake."

"Wow!" said Katie. "The Multiplier Effect makes Blowing Them Away an extremely powerful tool."

"You bet!"

"I have just a few more questions."

"Fire away."

"Are there other ways to blow people away besides writing notes to their bosses?"

"Yes, there are," responded Dr. Allen, "but I must say that recognition notes to bosses are probably the easiest and most effective way of getting the job done. People don't get them all that often, so it feels absolutely wonderful when they do."

"What if you *are* the boss?"

"Excellent question," said Dr. Allen. "You can have the same impact by sending a recognition note to *your* boss, your boss's boss, the president of your company—and, by all means, don't forget to send a copy to the individual involved.

"You can also blow people away by recognizing them and their accomplishments at staff meetings and company-wide events. Another thing you can do is to personally introduce them to your boss while you explain how they went the extra mile for you. The possibilities are limited only by your imagination."

"Is it too late to blow Sheila away for the special favor she did for me last week?" asked Katie.

"Absolutely not!" responded Dr. Allen. "On Monday, send her boss that note that we talked about, copy the appropriate people, and watch what happens. And, if you really want to bowl her over, you might bring her some flowers, also."

"Great idea!" said Katie, "I can't wait until Monday morning. I think I'm really going to enjoy this week."

"Don't forget to call me next Friday with a progress report."

"I won't," said Katie. "Have a great weekend."

SEVEN!

AN EXCITED KATIE DROVE TO WORK on Monday morning. She saw the Blowing Them Away step of Dr. Allen's program as her ticket to becoming a successful supervisor once again. Over the weekend, Katie had taken the time to develop an extensive list of things that she could do to blow people away. She was eager to start building her personal army of advocates.

As Katie pulled into the MedSol parking lot, she couldn't wait to send Sheila's boss that recognition note, and she had started wondering who else she would blow away that week. Approaching the building entrance, she didn't need to visualize the portrait of her children to bring a smile to her face—it was already there!

Build an Army

After she exchanged greetings with Joe, she went straight to her office and composed the note to Sheila's supervisor, Bill Rogers. The note read:

Dear Mr. Rogers:

I am a supervisor in Human Resources, and I want you to know that I have never before worked with a person of Sheila Davis's caliber. Her sense of commitment and attention to detail are outstanding, and it shows in the quality of her work. On numerous occasions this past year, she has stayed late at work in order to deliver reports to me *ahead of schedule!* Just think how well off the rest of the company would be if everyone here had Sheila's work ethic. You are truly fortunate to have Sheila in your department, because people like her are few and far between.

Sincerely,
Katie Adams

She then made copies for Sheila, Bill Rogers's boss, and Chad Morrison, the company president. She was smiling to herself as she thought about how much Sheila was going to love this as she dropped the notes into the intracompany mailbox.

When she turned and looked out into her department area, Katie discovered that she had been too focused on

Sheila's note to notice all the physical changes that had taken place since Friday afternoon. Almost everything had been rearranged: tables, desks, computers, printers, filing cabinets, and so forth.

EXCITE-MENT IS CONTA-GIOUS

So is passion. If you're fired up about what you do, chances are that those around you will be, too!

At this point, Greg walked up and said, "What do you think of the changes, Katie?"

"Who did all this, and when did it happen?"

"Justin and I came in over the weekend with a couple of other guys from the department and moved things around," Greg said proudly.

"Are you telling me you did this on your own time?" said Katie, amazed.

"You bet!" said Greg.

"Why?" asked Katie.

"So we could hit the deck running this morning with those changes we told you about last Friday and start getting rid of that work backlog that's been hanging around our necks."

REVVED!

Katie knew immediately that she would have to figure out some special way to blow these guys away, but for right now a hearty thank you would have to hold them over. She looked at Greg and said, "Great job, Greg! I can't thank you guys enough," as she shook his hand. "Where's Justin, and who were the people that helped you?"

"Justin will be back in a few minutes," said Greg. "The others who helped were Todd and Travis."

Katie immediately went to Todd and Travis's work area and thanked them both for coming in over the weekend, and she did the same when she saw Justin. She was already thinking about what she could do that would blow those four guys away as she walked back to her office.

At noon, instead of eating lunch in the MedSol cafeteria, Katie drove to a flower shop and bought a bright bouquet of flowers for Sheila. When Katie took the flowers over to her work area, Sheila was nowhere to be found, so Katie left the bouquet on her desk along with a note:

Dear Sheila:
Thanks again for all the extra things you have done for me.

Have a great day,
Katie

Later that afternoon, Sheila's name showed up on the caller ID of Katie's ringing phone. "I'm on my way to a meeting, but I want you to know that the flowers are gorgeous! Thank you so much. You made my day."

"Glad you like them," said Katie as she noticed a feeling of internal warmth that she hadn't felt in a long time.

"Have a nice day," said Sheila as she began to terminate the call.

"You too," said Katie. Seeing how those flowers had made Sheila's day, Katie wondered how Sheila was going to feel when she found out about the note to her boss.

At midmorning on Wednesday, there was a knock on Katie's door. It was Sheila. She was all smiles. "Hi, Katie!" she said. "I just stopped by to say hello and to see how things are going for you. By the way, I love that outfit you are wearing."

"Thank you. It's very kind of you to say that," replied Katie. "And thanks again for getting that report finished a day early. It sure made my job easier, having that extra day."

"I was happy to do it for you," said Sheila. "*Is there anything else I can do for you?*"

ENGAGE PEOPLE BY INVOLVING EVERYONE

In today's hypercompetitive marketplace, you cannot afford to take anyone for granted or leave anyone on the bench. Consider an informal get-together to discuss a key issue or topic. The key is making sure that everyone has a voice in making suggestions on how things can be improved.

REVVED!

The Magical Words

Right away, Katie recognized the magical words that meant the Blowing Them Away step was working on Sheila. She reasoned that Sheila was so happy and excited because she knew about the note Katie had sent to her boss.

"As a matter of fact there is," Katie said to Sheila.

"Your wish is my command," said Sheila, still smiling. "Just tell me what you need."

"I hear that you're good friends with Chad Morrison," said Katie.

"Yes, I am," said Sheila, a tone of caution entering her voice at the mention of the MedSol president's name. "We go to the same church."

"Let me tell you what I'm thinking," said Katie. "There are four men who work for me who came in over the weekend, on their own time, to physically reorganize my department in order to make our work flow more efficiently. As far as I'm concerned, that's above and beyond the call of duty. I would like to express my appreciation in a very special way, by introducing them to our president while I explain to him how they went the extra mile for MedSol."

"That's a great idea, Katie!" Sheila said, her smile returning. "Chad absolutely loves doing things like that. Let me go back to my office and call him to see if he has any openings in his schedule."

"I'd really appreciate that," said Katie. "The whole thing should take less than 10 minutes."

"Consider it done," said Sheila. "I'll call you after I talk to him. Take care, Katie, and please let me know if there is anything else that I can do for you."

"You too," said Katie. "Thanks for stopping by."

LEAVE A TRAIL OF GRATITUDE

When people really hit one out of the park for you, or even if they do something simple but well-meaning, find a sincere way to express your appreciation.

Shortly after lunch, Katie's phone rang. It was Sheila. "Katie, I just spoke with Chad. He says he has some time at 8:30 tomorrow morning."

"Wonderful! Thank you so much, Sheila."

"You're welcome, Katie. He said he's looking forward to meeting all of you."

Late that afternoon, Katie ran into Greg out in her department area. "How are those new changes working out?" she asked.

"Even better than we expected," said Greg proudly. "The work is moving through our department much faster than it did before. Our work backlog is already starting to shrink."

"That's wonderful!" responded Katie. "Could I ask a favor of you, Greg?"

"Sure, Katie, what is it?"

"Would you please arrange a meeting with you, Justin, Todd, and Travis in my office at 8: 15 tomorrow morning?"

"No problem, Katie. What's up?"

"It's a surprise," smiled Katie. "I'll see you tomorrow."

"Have a nice evening, Katie."

"You too," said Katie.

EIGHT!

THE NEXT MORNING AT 8:15, all four men were assembled in Katie's office. "What's up?" asked Justin.

"As I told Greg yesterday, it's a surprise. Follow me," she said as she started walking down the hall. The four men were indeed surprised when several minutes later they arrived at the president's outer office. "We're here to see Mr. Morrison," Katie said to Gail, the president's executive assistant.

"You must be Katie Adams. Chad is expecting you. I'll let him know you're here."

The Multiplier Effect in Action

A few minutes later, in walked a smiling Chad Morrison, president of MedSol. "Good morning," he said as he shook hands with Katie and each of the members of her entourage while exchanging introductions. "What can I do for you?"

Katie proceeded to tell the story, lavishing praise and credit on the four young men.

"Tell me," the president said, "are the changes working?"

"You bet!" Greg said proudly.

"Even better than we expected," added Justin.

"That's the kind of dedication that has made our company what it is today, and the four of you are to be commended for your loyalty to MedSol. Rather than having you tell me about these changes now, why don't I come over to your department right after lunch tomorrow and you can show me firsthand."

"That would be fantastic!" said Greg.

"All right, then, I'll see you all tomorrow, and, by all means, keep up the good work."

"Will do, Mr. Morrison," replied an excited Justin on behalf of the group.

"Just call me Chad," the president responded with a smile. "That's what I answer to best."

The four young men were completely blown away by what had just happened, and it showed. They all wanted to talk at once about how to plan for Chad Morrison's visit to their department.

At this point, Greg, the informal leader of the group, turned to Katie and said, "It was very nice of you to do what you just did, and I'm sure I speak for all of us when I say thank you very much."

The other three men chimed in with more thanks.

That warm feeling once again came over Katie. She looked at the four men and said, "You guys went the extra mile, on your own time, to make our department more productive. That kind of work ethic is rare and deserves the attention of the president. It was the least I could do."

The four were elated when they returned to their department. They immediately proceeded to tell their coworkers what had happened, and the news of Chad Morrison's upcoming visit spread like wildfire.

Katie had never seen the excitement level in her department this high. She knew she was witnessing the Multiplier Effect of the Blowing Them Away step in action. It was exciting—and, for whatever reason, it felt like the right thing to do!

The More You Give, the More Comes Back

The next day at 1:15, there was a knock on Katie's office door. It was Sheila along with Chad Morrison. "Katie," said Chad, "before we go out into your department, I want you to know that what you did for those four young men yesterday was a very good thing. That doesn't happen nearly enough, and yet it's what creates the excitement that drives productivity and builds company loyalty. So, thank you, Katie, for serving as a positive role model for the other supervisors and managers at MedSol."

Katie was quite taken aback. What she had just heard made her feel really good, especially since it came from the president. She didn't realize it at the time, but Chad Morrison had just Blown Her Away.

"I told you he was a nice guy," said Sheila smiling.

Then Chad said, "How do you want to handle my visit to your department?"

"The four guys you met with yesterday have your visit all planned out. They will be taking you around and explaining things," replied Katie.

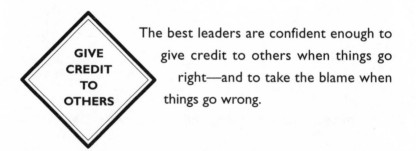

GIVE CREDIT TO OTHERS

The best leaders are confident enough to give credit to others when things go right—and to take the blame when things go wrong.

"While you stay in the background and let them take credit for their contributions?" suggested Chad. "I really like that in a supervisor. One of the things I have observed over the years is that successful bosses give away all the credit when things go well and absorb all the blame when things go badly. I think you have a really bright future here at MedSol, Katie. Keep up the good work."

"I'll do my best," Katie said proudly.

"Somehow, I know you will."

"Let me take you over to Greg, and we'll get your visit started."

Chad listened attentively as each of the four men proudly told him about his respective contribution to the department's reorganization. Chad also took the time to introduce himself and say something positive to every person in Katie's department.

As Katie observed Chad's behavior, she couldn't help but think to herself that he might also be using Dr. Allen's program.

When the visit was finished, Katie walked with Chad and Sheila to the edge of her department's area. "Thanks for taking the time, Chad. I know you are busy, but your visit really had an impact."

"The pleasure was all mine," he said as he shook Katie's hand. "Have a nice day, and, as I said earlier, keep up the good work."

Learn to Let Go

As Katie turned around and looked out over her department, she was happy with what she saw. The excitement level was high. The people seemed happy to be there, and they were working hard. Katie no longer felt the need to micromanage them. These people were doing fine on their own.

She couldn't wait to call the good doctor this afternoon. She had a lot to tell him.

On her way to her office, she ran into Sean McCarthy. "What was Morrison doing in your department?" he asked.

"Four of the guys who work for me came in over the weekend, on their own time, to rearrange my department to improve the work flow. Chad came by to look at the changes and to compliment them on their loyalty and dedication to MedSol."

"Interesting. Did he have anything to say to you?"

"As a matter of fact, he did. He thanked me for serving as a role model for other supervisors and managers at MedSol."

"Don't let it go to your head," he said dryly as he walked off.

"Have a nice weekend, Sean," she said warmly.

As usual, Sean did not respond. In Katie's mind, he didn't need to. She knew Sean well enough to know that he was assessing Chad Morrison's interest in her and her department only as it represented a threat to him. She wouldn't have been surprised if he was somehow planning to undermine her, but she was feeling too good to give it any thought.

DON'T LET 10 SECONDS RUIN YOUR DAY

Whether it is a put-down or a rude driver cutting you off in traffic, do not take it personally. Remember, you are in charge of your emotions!

At 2:15, she called Dr. Allen. Without realizing it, she accidentally conferenced Sean McCarthy into the call. Sean was in his office getting ready for his own conference call. When his phone rang, he pushed the speakerphone button and heard, "Hi, Dr. Allen, it's Katie from Deerfield."

Sean knew that this wasn't his conference call, but he continued to listen.

"Katie, it's so great to hear your voice!" said Dr. Allen. "Tell me, was it a good week?"

"It was a great week!"

"Tell me all about it."

"First of all, let me tell you that the Blowing Them Away step of your program is powerful stuff. There has never been as much excitement in my department as there is now. The people enjoy being here, they're working their tails off, and the quality of their work is off the charts—all because I *act* like I care about them. Let me tell you, this 'I am the master of my emotions' business is nothing short of amazing!"

"It sounds like the Multiplier Effect is starting to take hold in your department and your personal army of advocates is starting to grow."

"You bet!" said Katie. "As a result, I no longer feel like I have to micromanage—I'm actually starting to love being a supervisor again!"

"That's wonderful!" said Dr. Allen. "How did things go with Sheila?"

"Let me put it this way," said Katie. "I sent the letter to Sheila's boss on Monday, and she came into my office on Wednesday morning and uttered those magical words, '*Is there anything else I can do for you?*'"

"Well done, Katie! I'd say that you are already beginning to master the Blowing Them Away step of my program. Tell me, did anyone blow *you* away this past week?"

Katie thought for a moment and said, "It never occurred to me until now, but I was completely blown away by Chad Morrison, our company president."

"What happened?" asked Dr. Allen.

"In a nutshell, he told me that he liked the way I supervised, thanked me for serving as a positive role model for other managers and supervisors, and told me that I had a really bright future at my company."

"It sounds like everything's coming up roses for you, Katie, and that you are well on your way to becoming a superstar supervisor once again," said Dr. Allen.

"I'm actually starting to think so, too. I'm eager to learn what the third and final step of your program is all about."

"Before I give you the third step, I want you to focus on Blowing Them Away for two more weeks. This will make the third step that much more meaningful to you."

"Whatever you say, Dr. Allen. Have a nice weekend."

Katie had made arrangements to leave work early so that she could take her kids to the dentist. That turned out to be the perfect opportunity for Sean McCarthy to call an impromptu meeting of Katie's department.

NINE!

KATIE ARRIVED AT HER OFFICE on Monday morning to find a scowling Greg standing by the door with his arms folded across his chest. "Good morning, Greg," she said. "What's up?"

"Good morning, 'Katie from Deerfield,'" he said in a steely voice.

The Truth Comes Out

Katie felt as if she had just been punched in the stomach. Her heart pounded in her ears.

Greg surged on, "For the last two weeks, you have gone out of your way to convince everyone in our department that you cared about us—and we believed you! Sean overheard your phone conversation with Dr. Allen last Friday and told us that everything you did was just an act. He said you were boasting about how you got all of us to work hard for you by convincing us that you cared about us. Boy, do we feel used."

Greg was seething as he delivered the final blow. "Let me tell you, everyone in the department feels plenty ticked. Every last one is waiting in the conference room for a chance to nail you."

Katie was stunned and felt herself falter. She was afraid of going into the conference room and dealing with what must be an angry mob. She thought about crying, and she thought about going home. Then a voice inside her said, "The old Katie is back. She can handle this."

Katie paused, took a deep breath, looked at Greg and said, "Let's go."

Entering the conference room, Katie was met with a deafening silence and a sea of wounded-looking faces. Seeing how hurt and angry they all were made Katie's heart sink.

The awkward silence seemed to go on forever. Finally Greg asked slowly and deliberately, "What do you have to say to these people whom you've manipulated?"

Katie intently scanned the room, making eye contact with everyone. "The only thing I ask of you is that you hear my story before you make the decision whether or not to write me off," she said, her voice shaking.

"We'll give you that much," Greg said soberly.

REVVED!

Nothing Works Better Than the Truth

"As most of you remember, I used to be a successful supervisor. Then came personal problems, a divorce and betrayal that hurt me deeply—so much so that I never wanted to risk getting hurt like that again. So I distanced myself from everyone—my friends and my coworkers—and took my anger out on those around me. All this turned me into a lousy supervisor. That's when a good friend introduced me to Dr. Allen."

Katie took a deep breath and continued. "Dr. Allen told me that I had to care about the people around me if I expected to become a successful supervisor again. When I told him I couldn't because I was too afraid, he introduced me to a program that would enable me to *pretend* the caring part with no risk of being hurt. Because I was so desperate, I bought into his program hook, line, and sinker. What I didn't know at the time was that I was being manipulated by Dr. Allen."

"What do you mean?" asked Todd.

"Over the weekend I did some thinking about the turnaround of our department and how good I was feeling about things in general. It suddenly hit me that there is no such thing as pretending—either you care or you don't. You can't fake this stuff."

Katie paused to compose herself. "Yes, I came to work two weeks ago today thinking I was just going to pretend that I cared about you, but I failed miserably, and I'm glad I did. The truth is that what you have experienced these two weeks *is* the real Katie Adams, and she really *does* care about each and every one of you."

Katie's emotions finally took over and she started to cry. With tears rolling down her face she said, "You are all such wonderful people. I'm so very, very sorry."

There were few dry eyes left in the conference room. Greg picked up the box of tissues from the table in the front of the room and handed it to Katie. He then put his arm around her and said to the group, "I don't know about the rest of you, but after all that Katie's been through, I think she more than deserves another chance."

The group unanimously voiced its approval as the box of tissues began making its way around the room. A hug-fest quickly ensued. After a few minutes, Greg managed to get the group's attention and turned the floor over to Katie. By this time, she had regained some composure. "Thank you so much," she said smiling through a tear-streaked face. "I want you to know that I truly appreciate your support, and I promise that I will never let you down again."

As they left the conference room, each person came up to Katie and gave her a hug along with some personal words of encouragement. Instead of causing Katie's demise, as he had hoped to do, Sean McCarthy had inadvertently strengthened her bond with the people in her department. After everyone had left, Katie went back to her office to finish putting herself back together.

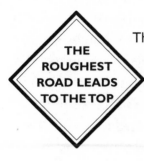

THE ROUGHEST ROAD LEADS TO THE TOP

This is because it's loaded with new challenges and experiences that enable you to learn, grow, and expand your comfort zone.

Turn the Other Cheek

At first Katie was extremely angry with Sean. She wanted to respond in kind and somehow make his life miserable. Then she remembered that the old Katie liked to bring out the best in people, not the worst.

Katie leaned back in her chair and reflected that people behave the way Sean did only if they're jealous or threatened. She decided to have a talk with him and find out what was going on—without letting things become confrontational.

Before heading over to the cafeteria to get a cup of coffee, Katie looked out over her department and liked what she saw—everyone was working hard with smiles on their faces. On her way back, she noticed Sean looking over a partition observing her department. She quietly walked up behind him and tapped him on the shoulder. Sean spun around with an expression of surprise and guilt on his face.

"What's the matter, Sean?" she asked, smiling. "Were you expecting to find my department in a shambles?"

"I don't know what you're talking about," Sean replied.

"You know exactly what I'm talking about," she said confidently. "I think we need to go into my office and talk."

As they entered her office, Katie closed the door. "Sean, you deliberately tried to sabotage me. That was a cruel thing to do, and very unwise, given the fact that you're my boss. If Jackie Peters or Chad Morrison were to find out about this, they would probably fire you on the spot."

"You've got me right where you want me, don't you?" he said cynically with his arms folded across his chest.

"No, Sean. I'm not into power games, and I would get no pleasure out of seeing you fired, but I do want to repair our relationship."

"Why would you want to do that?"

"Because I know that the way you have been treating me isn't the real you. When I first started working here, you and I became good friends, and we enjoyed working together. Then I got promoted and you didn't. Since then, you have been hostile toward me. Sean, I want you to be frank. What happened?"

Sean paused and then said, "Look, Katie, I wanted that promotion just as badly as you did, and I thought I deserved it. Then, when you went off the deep end and started acting like a 'Witch on Steroids,' I saw to it that Jackie Peters noticed."

"And then you got the promotion that was going to go to me. But why do you still continue to stab me in the back whenever you get a chance?"

"To keep the old Katie Adams from coming back. There is one more thing you may not realize—my other four departments are not doing anywhere near as well as yours. This makes you look good as a supervisor and me look bad as a manager. I'll be up front with you, Katie; I wanted you out of here."

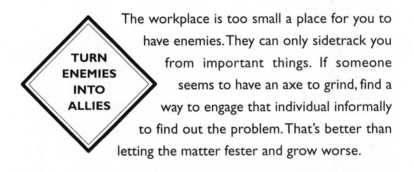

TURN ENEMIES INTO ALLIES

The workplace is too small a place for you to have enemies. They can only sidetrack you from important things. If someone seems to have an axe to grind, find a way to engage that individual informally to find out the problem. That's better than letting the matter fester and grow worse.

"I'm beginning to appreciate why you behaved the way you did," Katie said. "That being said, I think it's time for us to bury the competitive hatchet and start working together again."

"What do you mean?"

"During the last two weeks, I have learned a lot from Dr. Allen, starting with how to show people that I truly care about them."

"Didn't he teach you how to manipulate people by *pretending* that you cared about them?"

"As it turns out, he really didn't." Katie explained to Sean the series of events she had just described in the conference room.

"So *he* manipulated *you?*"

"That's what it looks like. But the fact of the matter is that the old me is back, and I would like to help you get those four departments shaped up so that you look like a superstar as a manager."

Sean was taken aback. "You'd do that after what I just tried to do to you?"

"Sean, we used to be good friends. I would like us to be good friends again, and that's what friends are for."

Sean looked at Katie. "You are being so good about things. I feel absolutely awful about the horrible way that I've been treating you. Please accept my apology. I am so sorry."

"No problem," she said as they exchanged hugs. "It's going to be fun working *together* again."

"So, when can we get started?"

"How about tomorrow morning?" she asked, smiling.

Clearing the Air

After Sean left her office, the nagging feeling that she had been manipulated by Dr. Allen resurfaced. She wanted to find out what was really going on, and to get his advice on how to help Sean, but she didn't want to do it when people from work could be listening. She wondered whether he would agree to meet in person.

Shortly after lunch, Katie decided to call Dr. Allen. "Hi, Katie! It's great to hear from you. How are things going?"

"Very well," said Katie.

"What can I do for you?" he asked.

"I was wondering if it would be possible to talk to you in person."

"Is there something wrong?"

"Well, as it turns out, one of the people at work over-heard our conversation last Friday."

"I hope that hasn't caused any problems for you."

"Oh, no! In fact, I think it has solved a major problem. But if it's possible, I would like to set up a meeting with you to discuss a couple of issues without the possibility of any people from work listening in."

"I completely understand. Where would you like to meet?"

"Are you familiar with the Carpe Diem Café?" Katie asked.

"I know where it is."

"How about tonight at 7:30?"

"That works for me," he said. "I'll be wearing a blue blazer with a red tie."

"Dr. Allen, I've seen your picture on the side of enough buses that I don't think I'll have any problem finding you. I'll be wearing a red leather jacket."

REVVED!

"Well, then, I'll see you tonight."

"I want you to know that I really appreciate your willingness to do this. Have a nice day."

"Katie, the pleasure is all mine. You have a nice day also."

TEN!

Face-to-Face Finally

Katie couldn't help noticing how excited she was about her meeting on the drive over to the café. As she entered, she recognized Dr. Allen at a corner table. He stood up to greet her as she approached.

"You must be Katie," he said, reaching to shake her hand.

"Let's see," she said with a smile, "blue blazer, red tie, and a recognizable face—you must be Dr. Allen."

"Please call me Michael," he said as he came around to take Katie's jacket and help her with her chair. Katie was immediately impressed. They ordered their favorite lattes and proceeded to get acquainted.

After they had conversed for a while, Katie leaned across the table and said, "Would you mind if I asked you a question about your program?"

"Absolutely not. Go right ahead."

"You've been deliberately manipulating me, haven't you?"

Michael was caught off guard. He paused and then said with a sheepish look on his face, "Yes I have—but let me assure you that my intentions were honorable."

"What do you mean?" asked Katie.

"Jennifer told me that before your divorce, you were a delightful, loving, happy, and caring individual whom everyone liked. Then you had to endure a series of awful experiences when your husband divorced you, married one of your friends, and moved to Italy, leaving you with no child support. The hurt you felt was so deep that you never wanted to experience it again. So, in the interest of protecting yourself, you became a person whom no one liked, including yourself."

"You've got that right," said Katie.

"My program was an attempt to trick you into caring about people again without the fear of being hurt. I thought that if you could feel what it's like to care about people once again and experience the love and caring that comes back when you do, you just might come back to being your old self."

"So you admit that your program is a sham?" she asked, tongue-in-cheek.

"I did try to trick you, but let me assure you that my program is no sham—it's actually called 'Looking Out for Number Two.'"

"I've heard the expression 'looking out for number one' before, but I've never heard of Looking Out for Number Two. What's the difference?"

"Looking out for number one is what you did when you focused only on yourself, trusted no one, and micromanaged those around you. How far did that get you?"

"It nearly cost me my job, not to mention some of my dearest friends."

"Then you started Looking Out for Number Two by engaging in the caring behaviors associated with Winning Them Over and Blowing Them Away, and look what happened."

"What I hear you saying, Michael, is that Looking Out for Number Two actually *is* taking care of number one."

"Well put," said Michael.

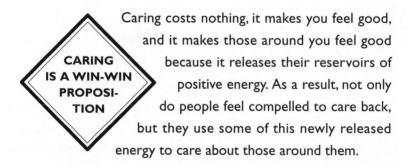

CARING IS A WIN-WIN PROPOSITION Caring costs nothing, it makes you feel good, and it makes those around you feel good because it releases their reservoirs of positive energy. As a result, not only do people feel compelled to care back, but they use some of this newly released energy to care about those around them.

"I think I see where this is going," said Katie, with a grin on her face. "When you care about people, they care back. This not only makes you feel good, but really good things start to happen to you as well."

"That's right."

"I must admit, your act was convincing. You really had me going," Katie said, laughing.

Michael then leaned forward across the table and said, "Katie, I hope you can forgive me."

"Are you kidding? Because of you, I've got my old life back. I haven't been this happy in a long, long time, and for that I thank you."

"The pleasure was all mine."

"There are a couple of additional things I would like to talk to you about."

"Fire away."

"My boss is the person who overheard our last phone conversation. He tried to sabotage me by telling the people in my department that I was manipulating them and that I really didn't care about them. When I arrived at work this morning, everyone was so upset that they were ready to lynch me."

"Oh, no! Katie, I'm so sorry if I—"

"There's nothing to apologize for. Fortunately for me, over the weekend, I saw through your program and realized that the old, caring Katie was definitely back. So I stood up in front of my department and told them the truth."

"How did they respond?"

"They all rallied around me. I truly feel that my relationships with the people in my department are stronger than they were before the incident occurred."

"The truth has a way of doing that," replied Michael. "But why would your boss do such a thing?"

"It turns out that my department is the only one of his five departments that is doing well. He said that made me look good as a supervisor and made him look bad as a manager."

"So, he was threatened by your success."

"Exactly."

"What happened next?"

"To make a long story short, I offered him an olive branch and told him I wanted to be friends again like we used to be. I offered to help him shape up his other four departments so that he would look like a superstar as a manager."

"I must say you *have* turned your life around. Most people would have a difficult time making such an offer, given what he had just tried to do to you. How did he respond?"

"He apologized, and he's very excited. We're meeting tomorrow morning. Do you have any suggestions on how I should proceed?"

"Just put him through the program the same way I did with you, one step at a time. Have him practice Winning Them Over and Blowing Them Away with everyone he comes into contact with—especially the supervisors of the other four departments."

"That's kind of what I thought," said Katie, "but I needed to hear it from you."

"I understand."

"I would like to meet with you again soon, to discuss how things are going with Sean."

"The last time we talked, you were going to call me a week from this Friday to learn about the third step in my program. Why don't we meet right here and discuss it then?"

"That sounds great. Is 7:30 a good time for you?"

"It works perfectly."

The rest of the evening flew by as Katie and Michael enjoyed each other's company. "Oh, my," said Katie, looking at her watch, "I don't know where the time went, but it's nearly 9:30. My kids are due home at 10:00, and I want to be there when they get home. As much as I hate to, I really must be going."

On her drive back home, Katie couldn't stop thinking about what a gentleman Dr.—Michael—had turned out to be. She wondered if this was the beginning of something special. It sure felt like it.

ELEVEN!

AT 8:30 THE NEXT MORNING, Sean arrived at Katie's office. "Come in," said Katie, "and have a seat."

"I want you to know that I really appreciate your taking the time to help me."

"Sean, believe me when I say that the pleasure is all mine. By the way, I met with Dr. Allen last evening and got a few things cleared up. As I suspected, his program is not about pretending, but about truly caring for those around you.

"It's called 'Looking Out for Number Two.' I also asked for his advice on how I should go about helping you. He said that I should put you through the same steps that he put me through."

"I'm ready when you are," he said eagerly, his pen and notepad in hand.

"Sean, some of the things I'm about to tell you may come across as simplistic, trivial, or even counterintuitive, but they work like nothing else does. You're going to have to take what I'm about to give you on blind faith until you experience the results. Trust me, they're off the charts!"

"Katie, you're a true friend. Why else would you be going to all of this extra effort for someone who just tried to sabotage you?"

Katie smiled. "Keep in mind that Looking Out for Number Two is all about caring for those around you. People will go the extra mile to help you succeed as a manager only if they're convinced that you care about them. As I found out, this is not something you can pretend; you have to be genuine."

"I'm ready to give it a shot, because I really want to succeed as a manager."

"Good, then let's get started. The first step of Dr. Allen's Looking Out for Number Two program is called Winning Them Over. The goal of this step is to turn the people you work with into loyal allies who are eager to support you in your role as a manager." Katie then proceeded to fill Sean in on the particulars of this step.

When she finished, Sean said, "Katie, this isn't going to be easy for me. I'm not used to behaving like this."

"What makes you think it was easy for me? Remember, I was the 'Witch on Steroids.' On the other hand, you've seen the impact this program has had on my department."

"Yes, I have, and it's impressive."

"If you want to achieve similar results as a manager, this is what you're going to have to do. Believe me, you're going to enjoy the ride.

"You might consider going back to your office and developing a personal action plan for handling each of these situations when they come up. Then, when you're finished, walk out of your office and start executing."

"Sounds like a plan," he said as he got up from his chair. "Thanks again, and have a great day."

"You too, Sean."

Sean got up, but as he reached the door, he turned and said with a chuckle, "Katie, I have to confess. I was the one who came up with the name 'Witch on Steroids.'"

Katie smiled as she said, "In hindsight, I think the name pretty much said what I was. See you on Friday."

CAPITALIZE ON MOMENTS OF TRUTH

A moment of truth is an opportunity to come through when the people around you don't expect you to. Think of ways to do this for colleagues and coworkers. You'll earn the respect of those around you, and the next time you ask one of these people for a favor, you can bet that the answer will be an enthusiastic yes!

REVVED!

The New and Improved Sean

On Friday afternoon at 2:30, Sean was parked outside Katie's office with a big smile on his face.

"Come in and tell me how it went."

"Well, I must admit that I didn't have a whole lot of faith in Dr. Allen's program when I left here on Tuesday. The only thing that prodded me into giving it a try was that I could see how well it is working for you."

"And?"

"Katie, this program is awesome! I can't believe how well it works. And so fast! I mean, it's only been four days, and already I've noticed some major changes."

"Like what?"

"People who used to walk the other way when they saw me coming down the hall now greet me with a smile and say something like: 'How's it going, Sean?' They also tell me to have a nice day when we part company. One of the other supervisors has already come to me with suggestions on how to increase her department's productivity, and another has voluntarily taken on more responsibility. I can't wait to learn about the next step in Dr. Allen's program!"

"It sounds like you're hooked, Sean."

"You bet!"

"So, how do you feel when you're acting this way?"

"I have to admit, it makes me feel really good, which makes the whole process a lot of fun."

"Well," said Katie smiling, "if you liked what resulted from Winning Them Over, you're really going to like the next step in Dr. Allen's program. It's called Blowing Them Away."

"It sounds interesting. What's it about?"

"The people you work with, especially the other four supervisors who report to you, are starting to get the message that you care about them. So, they are becoming excited about working hard to help you become a successful manager."

"How do you know this?"

"The two supervisors you just mentioned wouldn't have made those suggestions on how to improve things or volunteered to take on more responsibility if it didn't make them feel good. That tells you they're excited.

"The goal of Blowing Them Away is to take that excitement to the next level. You do this by singling out the people who have just gone the extra mile for you—like those two supervisors—and then blowing them away with the way you express your appreciation. The name of the game when it comes to blowing people away is to make them feel so good that they can't wait for an opportunity to do something for you again."

Katie then explained the details of Blowing Them Away, including the magical phrase that tells you that the step is working: "*Is there anything else I can do for you?*"

"Blowing Them Away sounds exciting! I can't wait for Monday to come around so I can start doing it."

REVVED!

"Do you want to get together next Friday afternoon to discuss how things are going?"

"You bet, Katie. Have a great weekend."

"You too, Sean."

The following week at work just breezed by, and on Friday afternoon Sean was standing in Katie's office doorway with an even bigger smile than the week before. "Katie, I can't believe how powerful this Blowing Them Away business is. The other supervisors are taking initiative like never before, constantly bombarding me with suggestions for improvement and smiling while they're doing it. I absolutely love this program!"

"It sounds like things are starting to go very well for you, Sean."

"They sure are. At this point, I have to admit that I'm really eager to learn what the third step of Dr. Allen's program is all about. When are you going to tell me?"

"To be honest, I don't know what it is myself, but I'm meeting with Dr. Allen tonight to find out. Why don't we get together the first thing on Monday morning, and I'll fill you in."

"That sounds perfect. Have a nice weekend."

"You have a nice weekend, too."

TWELVE!

AT 7:30 THAT EVENING, Katie walked into the Carpe Diem Café. She saw Michael sitting at the same table as before.

"Hi, Katie," he said as he helped her off with her coat.

"Judging from your choice of tables, I'm guessing that you are a creature of habit," she said, smiling.

"Perhaps," he said as he hung her coat over a vacant chair. "Or maybe I made a conscious decision to the effect of, 'If something isn't broken, don't fix it.'"

The two looked at each other and laughed.

"Katie, I am eager to hear how things have gone with Sean."

"In a word, he's hooked! He is so pleased with the results of his doing the first two steps of your program that he's beside himself."

"That's great!"

"Both of us are dying to learn about the third step of your program."

"Excellent!" he said, clearly delighted with what he was hearing. Michael paused for a few seconds. He then looked at Katie and said, "The third and final step in my program is called, *Keeping Them Revved.*"

"Let's see if I can figure this step out on my own," said Katie. "The first step is about getting people excited about working hard again, and the second takes that excitement to the next level. So, Keeping Them Revved must be about keeping that excitement at the next level indefinitely."

"You are a quick study, Katie. No wonder you've come such a long way in just four weeks."

"I have to admit that your program has taken me well beyond my original expectations."

"Hearing you say that makes my day."

"What does Keeping Them Revved involve?"

"It involves making sure that you *continue* to do those things that are necessary to win people over and blow them away on a consistent basis, day in and day out. You have to remember that you are dealing with people. People are sensitive; they have delicate egos, and they need to feel good about themselves. As a result, they absolutely hate being jerked around."

"Jerked around? What do you mean by that?"

"That's what you're doing if you go through the motions of Winning Them Over and Blowing Them Away when you want their help, then ignore them until you want their help again. This sends a clear message that you are taking them for granted or using them, which tells them that you really don't care. When people get this message, they lose interest in going the extra mile for you and take their best efforts somewhere else where they are better appreciated."

"What I hear you telling me is that if I were inconsistent in my efforts at Winning Them Over and Blowing Them Away, it would be extremely difficult for me to be a successful supervisor."

"More like impossible," said Michael. "As I said before, it simply can't happen unless the people around you are convinced that you truly care about them."

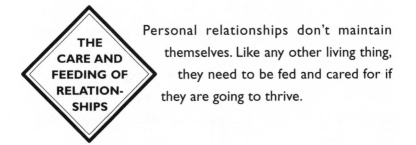

THE CARE AND FEEDING OF RELATIONSHIPS

Personal relationships don't maintain themselves. Like any other living thing, they need to be fed and cared for if they are going to thrive.

"How do I make sure that I do these necessary things on a consistent basis, day in and day out?" asked Katie.

"By making Looking Out for Number Two *a way of life*," replied Michael.

"How do I do that?"

"By practicing Winning Them Over and Blowing Them Away with *everyone* you come into contact with, not just the people at work. I'm talking about the checkout clerk at the grocery store, the customer service person at the dry cleaners, the sales staff at the department store, tellers at the bank, the mail person, and your neighbors."

"Will the people I care about outside of work become part of my personal army of advocates too?"

"Absolutely! While a salesperson at a department store or a bank teller may not be able to do much to help your work situation, there are lots of things he or she can do to make your life easier and more enjoyable."

"What kinds of things?"

"Well, here's an example for starters. I knew this woman—Margie—who took the time to get to know one of the salespeople at her favorite department store. After she had received exceptional service from this woman several times, Margie wrote the woman's boss a note telling him what a great employee he had. Margie also sent copies to the store manager, the president of the chain, and the salesperson.

"A month or so later, she was in the store and getting ready to buy several expensive outfits when this salesperson told her that the store was having an unannounced sale the next day, and everything was going to be 50 percent off! She then offered to set those outfits aside for a day if Margie wanted come back and take advantage of the sale price."

"That's wonderful."

"Hold on, Katie, there's more. When a new shipment of clothing comes into the store, if it contains an outfit that the salesperson thinks Margie would like, she calls and offers to hold one in her size until Margie can come to the store and check it out."

"That's really amazing," said Katie. "I can't wait to share this with Sean. When should we get together again—next week?"

"This time I want you to wait four weeks. Then I want you to call me and set up a meeting so we can discuss how your entire life has changed for the better."

"Will do," said Katie.

With the business part of their meeting concluded, they each ordered a glass of wine and proceeded to get better acquainted. Katie thoroughly enjoyed Michael's company and couldn't believe how much they had in common. At 9:30, she said, "I really hate to break up this wonderful evening, but I have to pick up my daughter and her friend from a school play."

"I hate to see it end, too, but I understand how important your kids are to you. Some day I would like to meet them."

"Some day," she said, smiling.

THIRTEEN!

ON MONDAY MORNING, Katie met with Sean and explained the Keeping Them Revved step of Dr. Allen's program to him. When she told him it was all about making Looking Out for Number Two a way of life, his response was, "That's kind of what I thought it would be, because it's the only thing that makes sense."

During the next four weeks, Katie never missed an opportunity to practice Looking Out for Number Two, and the results began to snowball. It seemed like every place she went, people were greeting her with, "Hi, Katie; is there anything I can do for you?" Her neighbors and old friends were inviting her to parties again.

Nowhere were the results more evident than at work. When the monthly supervisor rankings were released, Katie was once again ranked at the top. Her department was also rated number one in terms of morale and productivity. Things were going so well that she felt as if her life were on cruise control.

On the fourth Friday afternoon, Katie leaned back in her office chair, enjoying how good it was to be on top of things again. She had made arrangements to meet with Michael that evening, and she was excited about getting together with him. *I have so much to tell him,* she thought.

Just then there was a knock on her office door. It was Jackie and Sean. "I must say you've had quite a month!" said Jackie. "It looks to me like we have the old Katie Adams back."

"You sure do!" Katie said with a grin. "Things are definitely going well."

"Congratulations on your accomplishments," Jackie continued. "I want to be the first to tell you that if you keep this up, we will be talking about promotion opportunities real soon."

"Thank you for saying that, Jackie. It means a lot to me."

"Sean has also filled me in on how you helped him become a better manager. Each of his other four departments has made a dramatic turnaround."

"Thank you for the kudos, Sean."

"Katie, that's the least I could do given all that you have done for me. As I've said before, you are a true friend."

"Have a nice weekend," they both said as they began to leave.

"And, once again," Jackie said, "welcome back."

"Thanks again," said Katie. She couldn't imagine things getting any better than they were at that moment.

A few minutes later, there was another knock on her office door. This time it was Chris Thomas, the vice president of human resources, and Chad Morrison, the president of MedSol!

Katie was surprised. "Are you two lost?" she asked, tongue-in-cheek.

"Not at all," replied Chris. "We're here to see you."

"Well, then," said Katie, "come on in and have a seat. What can I do for you?"

"Chad and I have been watching your department with great interest ever since Chad came to see the changes those four guys made over the weekend on their own time. We have both concluded that we have never seen people work harder while enjoying it more, and we've never seen such a fast, complete turnaround.

"Chad and I think you're onto something big that could really benefit MedSol. Katie, we'd like to offer you a position on our corporate staff as the director of human potential. The position would involve capturing what you're doing as a supervisor and documenting it, developing education programs that will teach managers and supervisors how to do what you're doing and achieve what you're achieving, and then monitoring their progress. This position also involves a pay increase of several grades."

"Are you interested, Katie?" asked Chad.

"You bet I am!" said Katie. "This is wonderful! The two of you have really made my day."

"No, Katie," said Chad, "you've made ours. Why don't you stop by my office on Monday morning at 9:30, and the three of us will talk further about your new position. In the meantime, enjoy your weekend," he said as he shook Katie's hand, "and welcome to the corporate staff."

"The same goes for me," said Chris as she extended her hand to Katie. "Welcome aboard."

"Thank you both so much for this opportunity."

"See you on Monday," said Chad.

Katie was ecstatic. *I really can't believe what's happening,* she thought.

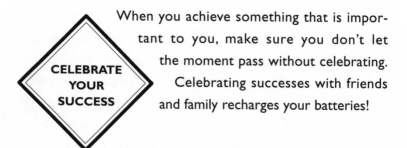

CELEBRATE YOUR SUCCESS

When you achieve something that is important to you, make sure you don't let the moment pass without celebrating. Celebrating successes with friends and family recharges your batteries!

FOURTEEN!

WHEN KATIE WALKED INTO the Carpe Diem Café that evening, she saw Michael sitting at a table by the fireplace instead of the usual one in the corner.

"What happened to our creature of habit?" she asked when she got to the table. "Did he get lost?"

"Maybe he thought it was time for a change of scenery," he said with a chuckle as he helped her off with her coat.

"So tell me, Katie, how has your life been these past four weeks?" Michael continued.

"Unbelievable!" replied Katie. "Absolutely unbelievable! I don't see how things could get much better."

"How does all this make you feel?"

"That's an interesting question. I haven't really thought about it all that much because things have been so busy, but I have to say that I haven't felt this good or this happy since before my ex-husband asked for a divorce. I don't know how I can ever thank you for making all this possible."

"Just hearing that you have your life back on track is thanks enough for me."

"Do you know what most amazes me about all of this?" Katie continued.

"What?"

"How much your life can change for the better in a *very* short period of time when you start caring about the people around you. I mean, the payoff is mind-boggling."

"It makes you wonder why more people don't make caring a way of life, doesn't it?"

"I was just going to say that. Why *don't* more people make caring for others a way of life? It's so simple, it requires so little effort, and the payoff, in terms of making your work life and personal life better, is enormous."

"The reason is that most people don't realize there *is* a payoff associated with caring about others. They see activities such as listening to people and writing their bosses recognition notes only in terms of their spending time and energy to benefit someone else. Given the choice, most people would rather spend their time and energy doing things they think will benefit *themselves*. So that's what they do."

"What I think you're saying is that there would be a lot more highly successful people if they only understood that *looking out for others is really looking out for yourself*."

"You've got that right."

REVVED!

Katie paused for a moment to sit with the powerful truth of her deceptively simple realization. Suddenly, it occurred to her that her work with Dr. Allen might be finished—a development that she wasn't ready to accept.

"Where do we go from here?" she asked. "Is there anything else that I need to learn about your program?"

"Not really. As far as I can tell, you've mastered all three steps: Winning Them Over, Blowing Them Away, and Keeping Them Revved. I hate to sound like a mother eagle, Katie, but you're ready to leave the nest."

"Does this mean I don't get to meet with you anymore?"

"Hardly. What it does mean is that we can meet for reasons other than to discuss my program. How about dinner and a movie?" he said in his smooth radio voice.

FIFTEEN!

One of Life's Most Important Lessons

As director of human potential at MedSol, Katie became the company champion of Dr. Allen's Looking Out for Number Two program. She made sure that everyone understood the tangible benefits associated with caring. Within a year, she had every department practicing the caring behaviors included in the program's three steps:

- Winning Them Over
- Blowing Them Away
- Keeping Them Revved

The payoff for MedSol was phenomenal. Morale and productivity improved dramatically, and turnover declined.

REVVED!

MedSol became known as a fun place to work, and the Human Resources department was constantly being bombarded with employment applications from people who wanted to work there.

MedSol was made up of the same people as before, with the same buildings and the same products. The only difference was that now, from top to bottom, the people at MedSol cared about one another, and they let it show.

At no time was this more apparent than at a celebration that happened to coincide with Katie's one-year anniversary in her new position—an early spring afternoon on which it seemed that most of MedSol had showed up to watch Michael and Katie become husband and wife. Katie's colleagues were delighted to welcome Dr. Allen into the MedSol family—for thanks to him, they had learned one of life's most important lessons:

Looking out for number two is really taking care of number one.

REVVED!

Group Discussion Questions

The following questions may be used to stimulate lively group discussion about *REVVED!*:

Winning Them Over

1. What is the goal of *Winning Them Over*? What does it involve?
2. Why is it important to have a smile on your face when you're trying to win someone over?
3. Give some examples of nice or positive things you can say to people as you greet them.
4. What does *active listening* involve?
5. Why is active listening so important when it comes to winning people over?
6. Share some examples of how you've won people over or how people have won you over.

Blowing Them Away

1. What is the goal of *Blowing Them Away?*
2. What does *Blowing Them Away* involve?
3. Why doesn't a simple "thank you" via email or a thank you note blow people away?

4. What is the magical phrase that tells you the *Blowing Them Away* step is working?
5. What is the *Multiplier Effect?*
6. What does the *Multiplier Effect* enable you to build?
7. Share some examples of how you have blown people away or how you've been blown away.

Keeping Them Revved!

1. What is the goal of *Keeping Them Revved!?*
2. What does *Keeping Them Revved!* involve?
3. Why is *Keeping Them Revved!* so important?
4. How do you make sure that you do those things necessary to *Win Them Over* and *Blow Them Away* on a consistent basis, day in and day out?
5. Will the people in your personal life with whom you practice *Winning Them Over* and *Blowing Them Away* become part of your *personal army of advocates*? Share some examples.
6. What does the phrase *"looking out for number two is really taking care of number one"* mean?

A Five-Day *REVVED!* Action Plan

REVVED! is about reaching out and letting people know you care about them. In order for *REVVED!* to work, you have to be genuine and sincere with no hidden agenda.

DAY 1 *Winning Them Over*—Be Positive and Upbeat

Remember, the goal of *Winning Them Over* is to get those around you at work *excited* about going the extra mile for you. You do this by engaging in the following behaviors:

Smiling—a smile has such a profound positive impact on people that it is the one thing that is used more than sex in advertising. Before you get out of bed in the morning, make up your mind that you are going to wear a smile that makes you look like one of the happiest people in the world.

Saying something positive—cheerfully greet everyone you come into contact with and have something positive to say to them. (Examples: "Good morning!" "How are you today?" "You look very nice today." "I love your sweater.") Also, use the phrase "thank you" whenever you can.

DAY 2 *Winning Them Over*—Show a Genuine Interest

Actively engage—in addition to smiling and saying something positive, actively engage the people you come into contact with. For example, ask them how things are going. And when they answer, *actively listen* to what they have to say.

Actively listen—stop what you're doing and focus solely on what these people have to say and nothing else—no looking at your watch, reading your e-mail or any other form of multitasking while they're talking to you. Also, ask a few questions about what they're saying. Do the same thing when people come to you with a question or a problem.

DAY 3 *Blowing Them Away*

Remember, the goal of **Blowing Them Away** is to take the excitement created by **Winning Them Over** to the *next level*. You do this by engaging in the following behaviors:

Singling them out—identify those people who have just gone the extra mile for you.

Blowing them away with your expression of appreciation—do it in such a manner that makes people feel so great for having gone the extra mile for you that they can't wait for a chance to do it again. For example, send a thank-you note to the person's boss and boss's boss. Be sure to copy the person who went the extra mile, and do it with hard copy, not e-mail.

REVVED!

DAY 4 *Keeping Them Revved!*

Remember, the goal of *Keeping Them Revved!* is to keep the excitement at the next level *indefinitely*. You do this by practicing **Winning Them Over** and **Blowing Them Away** with *everyone* you come into contact with, not just the people at work. This includes the checkout clerk at the grocery store, the customer service person at the dry cleaners, the sales staff at the department store, tellers at the bank, the mail person, and your neighbors.

DAY 5 *Enjoy!*

As you continue to do the things necessary to **Win Them Over** and **Blow Them Away**, take note of how great all this makes you feel and how much easier your life has become. Notice how often you begin to hear those magical words—*Is there anything else I can do for you?*—which tell you that **REVVED!** is working for you. That's it. You're on your way. Keep doing what you're doing, and watch your *personal army of advocates* begin to grow.

For more information on getting your team **REVVED!**, visit www.revvedbook.com.

ABOUT THE AUTHORS

Harry Paul has more than 20 years of first-hand knowledge in running all aspects of a management training and consulting business, including sales, distribution, product development, and international operations.

He has served as a senior vice president for The Ken Blanchard Companies, where he personally managed the speaking career of Dr. Kenneth Blanchard, coauthor of *The One Minute Manager*. Previously he owned and managed his own printing and publishing company.

Harry is coauthor of four internationally best-selling business books, including *FISH! A Remarkable Way to Boost Morale and Improve Result.*

Harry lives in Poway, California with his wife and two children.

For information regarding Harry Paul's speaking availability, please call 760-212-8993 or e-mail thepauls@cox.net.

Ross Reck received his Ph.D. from Michigan State University in 1977. From 1975 to 1985 he served as Professor of Management at Arizona State University. During his career at ASU, he was the only two-time recipient of the prestigious Teaching Excellence in Continuing Education award and was identified by the university as an "Outstanding Teacher."

He is coauthor of the best-selling *The Win-Win Negotiator,* and author of *Turn Your Customers into Your Sales Force* and *The X-Factor.*

A compelling and dynamic speaker, Ross has been featured at hundreds of meetings, conferences, and conventions throughout the United States, Canada, Latin America, Europe, and Asia. His consulting clients include Hewlett-Packard, John Deere, American Express, Janssen-Ortho, Inc., the Chicago Cubs, and Xerox.

Ross resides in Tempe, Arizona with his wife and three children.

For information regarding Ross's speaking or consulting availability, call 602-391-3250 or go to www. rossreck.com.